ROBOTS EXPLORING SPACE

THE CASSINI MISSION

Robots Exploring Saturn and Its Moon Titan

Angela Royston

PowerKiDS
press

NEW YORK

Published in 2017 by **The Rosen Publishing Group**
29 East 21st Street, New York, NY 10010

Produced for Rosen by Calcium

Editors for Calcium: Sarah Eason and Harriet McGregor
Designers for Calcium: Jennie Child
Picture researcher: Rachel Blount

Picture credits: Cover: NASA/JPL (Cassini image), Thinkstock: Pixtum (top banner), Shutterstock:
Andrey_Kuzmin (metal plate), Thinkstock: -strizh- (back cover illustration); Inside: ESA: D. Ducros
20; NASA: Steven Hobbs (Brisbane, Queensland, Australia) 22–23, JPL-Caltech 24, JPL-Caltec h/
Space Science Institute 28, JPL/Space Science Institute 15, 19, 26, JPL/University of Colorado 16;
Shutterstock: 3000ad 9, Elenarts 4–5; Wikimedia Commons: David Monniaux (CC BY-SA 3.0) 11,
NASA 7, NASA/JPL/KSC 13.

CATALOGING-IN-PUBLICATION DATA
Names: Royston, Angela.
Title: The Cassini mission: robots exploring Saturn and its moon Titan / Angela Royston.
Description: New York : Powerkids Press, 2017. | Series: Robots exploring space | Includes index.
Identifiers: ISBN 9781508151357 (pbk.) | ISBN 9781508151296 (library bound) |
    ISBN 9781508151180 (6 pack)
Subjects: LCSH: Saturn (Planet)--Juvenile literature. | Saturn (Planet)--Exploration--
    Juvenile literature.
Classification: LCC QB671.R68 2017 | DDC 523.46--dc23

Manufactured in the United States of America
CPSIA Compliance Information: Batch #BS16PK. For Further Information contact Rosen Publishing, New York, New York at 1-800-237-9932

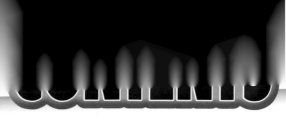

CONTENTS

The Mission

On October 15, 1997, spacecraft *Cassini*, with a separate **probe** called *Huygens* riding on its back, were blasted from Earth into space. Their mission was to explore the planet Saturn and its moons. There were no astronauts on board *Cassini*. Both *Cassini* and *Huygens* were **robots** programmed to carry out instructions.

Destination Saturn

Cassini was not the first unmanned robot spacecraft to visit Saturn. *Pioneer 11* and both *Voyagers 1* and *2* had already flown past it. So, although Saturn is at least 750 million miles (1.2 billion km) from Earth, scientists already knew quite a lot about this incredible planet. They knew it consisted mainly of **hydrogen** and is the second biggest planet in the solar system, after Jupiter. Saturn is circled by an extensive and amazing system of rings. Scientists had seen the rings through telescopes and from the latest photographs sent back to Earth by *Voyager*. At the time of the launch, 18 moons had been identified **orbiting** Saturn, but scientists suspected there were more.

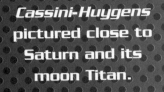

Cassini-Huygens pictured close to Saturn and its moon Titan.

The *Cassini-Huygens* mission had many ambitious objectives. Some related to Saturn's rings, some to its **atmosphere**, and many to its moons, particularly to Titan, the largest moon. For example, scientists wanted to know what lay hidden below Titan's thick atmosphere. They wanted to know where the materials that made up the rings had come from, and why they varied in color.

Unusual Moons

Many of the mission's objectives concerned Saturn's less well-known moons, including Enceladus and Iapetus, which has a very bright side and a side that always looks dark, even in daytime. Scientists wanted to know how old the moons are and what they consist of. In particular, scientists wanted to find out whether the conditions on any moon might support life.

Groundwork

The *Cassini-Huygens* mission took many years to plan and develop. In the 1980s, space scientists from the United States and from Europe met to talk about projects they might work on together. They shared a common ambition, which was to combine a large robot spacecraft that would orbit Saturn and its moons with a smaller robot probe that would land on Titan.

The combined spacecraft would be one of the largest, most complex spacecraft ever built, and the most expensive. The total cost of $3.26 billion was too much for any one organization to fund. So the National Aeronautics and Space Administration (NASA), which is the United States' space agency, and the European Space Agency (ESA) combined with the Italian Space Agency (ASI), to raise the money. Ultimately, NASA paid for 80 percent of the project, ESA 15 percent, and ASI paid 5 percent.

Who Built What

The three space agencies combined their skills to design and build the two spacecraft and all the equipment they carried. *Cassini*, the large **orbiter** spacecraft, was built in the United States by the Jet Propulsion Laboratory (JPL) working for NASA, while *Huygens*, the smaller probe, was developed and built in Europe, mostly in France. The ASI worked on the communications technology.

Most of the mission was planned and programmed before launch. Every problem had to be anticipated and solved in advance. After the launch, the project was managed by **mission control**, set up by JPL in Pasadena, California. Scientists monitored information received from *Cassini* and sent additional instructions to it.

Huygens is the gold-covered disk on the left of **Cassini**.

Huygens

SPACE FIRST

GALILEO GALILEI (1564–1642) WAS AN ITALIAN MATHEMATICIAN AND ASTRONOMER WHO, ON JULY 25, 1610, BECAME THE FIRST PERSON TO SEE SATURN IN THE NIGHT SKY. HE USED A TELESCOPE THAT HE HAD BUILT HIMSELF. IT ALLOWED GALILEO TO SEE A PLANET WITH WHAT LOOKED LIKE A SMALLER OBJECT ON EACH SIDE. ALTHOUGH GALILEO DID NOT REALIZE IT, THESE WERE ACTUALLY SATURN'S RINGS.

Lowdown on Cassini

Cassini is a large and impressive spacecraft. It is more than 22 feet (6.7 m) long, 13 feet (4 m) wide, and its boom is 36 feet (11 m) long. Its 12 special instruments can detect, photograph, and measure Saturn's atmosphere, rings, and moons.

Nuclear Power

A spacecraft needs electricity to run its **thruster engines**, computers, radio transmitters, and other instruments. Most spacecraft have solar panels, which are panels that use sunlight to produce electrical power. However, Saturn is too far from the sun to use solar panels. Instead, *Cassini*'s three **generators** use nuclear power. Each radioisotope thermoelectric generator (RTG) uses heat from radioactive plutonium pellets to generate electricity.

Cassini communicates with mission control and *Huygens* through its **antennae**. The large, round antenna at the top of the spacecraft is called a high-gain antenna because it can send

SPACE FIRST

SATURN IS SURROUNDED BY A MAGNETOSPHERE. THIS IS A FIELD OF MAGNETICALLY CHARGED **PARTICLES**, LIKE THOSE SURROUNDING EARTH, WHICH A COMPASS USES TO FIND NORTH. A MAGNETOMETER ON *CASSINI*'S BOOM ACTS AS A COMPASS TO HELP THE SPACECRAFT NAVIGATE AROUND SATURN AND ITS MOONS. INCREDIBLY, THE MAGNETOMETER CAN ALSO "SEE" INSIDE SATURN AND ITS MOONS TO HELP SCIENTISTS FIGURE OUT WHAT THEIR CORES ARE MADE OF.

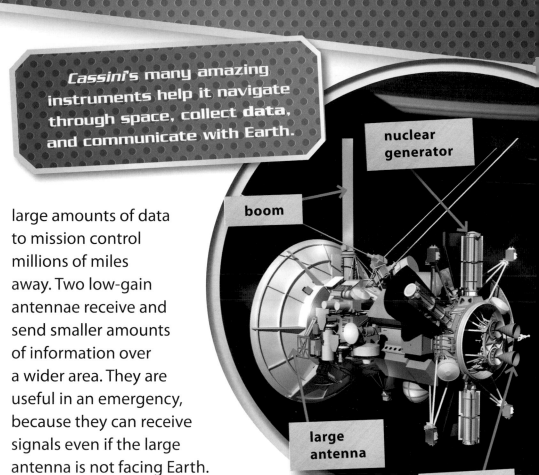

Cassini's many amazing instruments help it navigate through space, collect data, and communicate with Earth.

nuclear generator

boom

large antenna

thruster engines

large amounts of data to mission control millions of miles away. Two low-gain antennae receive and send smaller amounts of information over a wider area. They are useful in an emergency, because they can receive signals even if the large antenna is not facing Earth.

Super Sensors

Cassini's instruments are super **sensors**. They can, for example, detect a wider range of light than our eyes can, and feel particles that are too small for our fingertips to detect. A cosmic dust analyzer can tell what the tiny specks of dust in the atmosphere are made from. Instruments on *Cassini*'s fields and particles pallet also study dust and gases, while those on the remote sensing pallet use light to photograph Saturn, its rings, and moons. Instruments in the radar bay use radio waves to measure the size of particles in the rings and map the surface of Titan through its thick atmosphere.

Zoom-in to Huygens

Huygens is smaller and lighter than *Cassini*. It is 8.9 feet (2.7 m) across and weighs 769 pounds (349 kg), about one-sixth as much as *Cassini*. *Huygens* was designed and programmed to examine the atmosphere of Titan, Saturn's largest moon. Scientists knew that Titan's atmosphere is different from the air that surrounds Earth. To start with, it is bright orange! *Huygens* is equipped with scientific instruments to analyze different aspects of these thick orange gases.

Huygens consists of two parts, or modules. The Descent Module was designed to fall through Titan's atmosphere to land on its surface. This module has a hard outer shell, like a clam, and a heat shield to protect the scientific instruments inside. The Entry Assembly Module stays on *Cassini*. It controls the Descent Module, receives information and pictures beamed back to it, and passes them to *Cassini*.

SPACE FIRST

As soon as *Huygens* lands, the surface science package (SSP) goes into action. It has many different sensors and they transmit information about the ground the robot lands on. This gives scientists important information about the surface, including its temperature and whether the probe's landing site is liquid or solid.

A strong shell protects *Huygens's* instruments as it travels through space.

Two scientific instruments were designed to identify the chemicals that make up Titan's atmosphere. The gas chemical analyzer would take samples of air from 106 miles (170 km) above the ground down to the moon's surface, and use color and light waves to identify different gases. An aerosol collector would also sample the atmosphere. As part of this process, it would separate tiny floating particles, called aerosols, by pumping the samples through **filters** before analyzing them.

Wind, Sound, and Images

Three instruments would study the atmosphere. Scientists wanted to know more about Titan's weather system, so they included an instrument that measures the speed and direction of the wind at different heights above the ground. Another instrument records the temperature at different heights in the atmosphere, and has a microphone for picking up sounds on Titan. The Descent Imager and Spectral Radiometer (DISR) includes cameras that take colored images above, to the side, and below the probe.

Time to Go!

Cassini-Huygens was launched at night on October 15, 1997. It would not reach Saturn until nearly seven years later, on July 1, 2004. It was too far to fly directly to Saturn, so scientists programmed the robot spacecraft to boost its speed by looping twice around the sun and flying past Venus, Earth, and Jupiter on the way. This gave the spacecraft some of the planets' **momentum**, which provided as much power as an extra 75 tons (68 mt) of fuel.

Cassini-Huygens was assembled on top of a Titan-4B/Centaur rocket launcher, at Cape Canaveral in Florida. The rocket launcher and spacecraft were as high as a 20-story building! At 4:43 a.m. Eastern Daylight Time, Titan-4B fired up and the huge mass lifted off the ground and soared through the air into orbit around Earth.

Circling the Sun

Once in orbit, Centaur took over. Its rockets boosted Cassini-Huygens's speed and pushed the spacecraft out of Earth's orbit. The boosters fell away and the robot traveled past Venus and around the sun. To protect the instruments on board from the sun's heat, Cassini used its large antennae as a sunshade.

After flying again around the sun and past Venus, Cassini-Huygens flew past Earth before heading off to Jupiter, which it reached on December 30, 2000. The spacecraft was now halfway to Saturn. By flying close to the giant planet Jupiter, the spacecraft gained enough speed to take it to Saturn, which it reached nearly four years later, in 2004.

SPACE DISCOVERY

AS *CASSINI* FLEW PAST JUPITER, SCIENTISTS USED THE OPPORTUNITY TO TAKE A CLOSE LOOK AT IT. THE ROBOT'S CAMERAS TOOK 26,000 PICTURES OF JUPITER'S ATMOSPHERE AND BEAMED THEM BACK TO MISSION CONTROL. FOR THE FIRST TIME, SCIENTISTS WERE ABLE TO SEE CLEAR IMAGES OF BANDS OF WINDS CIRCLING THE PLANET AND A HUGE, SWIRLING DARK PATCH CLOSE TO JUPITER'S NORTH POLE.

Phoebe Flyby

Before *Cassini-Huygens* reached Saturn, it examined Phoebe, one of the planet's farthest moons. When scientists planned the mission they knew that Phoebe would be in a good position for *Cassini* to gain momentum from a **flyby**. At the same time, they wanted the space robot to find out more about this moon.

Phoebe

Phoebe is a solid moon about 8 million miles (13 million km) from Saturn. Scientists are interested in Phoebe because it orbits Saturn in the opposite direction to Titan and the other moons. Most moons were created from gas and dust soon after Saturn formed, but Phoebe was different. Sometimes **asteroids** or objects elsewhere in the solar system travel so close to a planet, they become captured, or trapped, in orbit around it. One of *Cassini*'s objectives was to collect data to help scientists find out what Phoebe was made of and where it came from.

Phoebe Flyby

On June 11, 2004, *Cassini* flew just 1,285 miles (2,068 km) away from Phoebe. The robot used some of its instruments to analyze the rocks and its remote sensing pallet to take closeup images of the moon's surface. Phoebe measures only 137 miles (220 km) across, so these instruments had to be carefully timed to collect as much data as possible.

Cassini's next task was to transmit the images and data to mission control on Earth. *Cassini*'s large antenna sent the files and they were picked up by NASA's Deep Space Network (DSN).

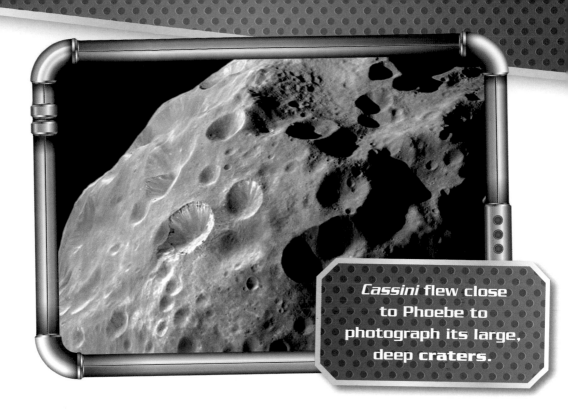

Cassini flew close to Phoebe to photograph its large, deep craters.

The Network consists of three very large and sensitive antennae that span the world: one in California, one in Spain, and the third in Australia. As Earth spins from day to night, there is always an antenna in contact with the spacecraft.

SPACE DISCOVERY

WHEN MISSION CONTROL RECEIVED THE FIRST CLOSEUP PICTURES OF PHOEBE, THEY COULD SEE AT ONCE THAT PHOEBE WAS NOT AN ASTEROID. USING ALL THE DATA SENT BY THE ROBOT, SCIENTISTS MADE A COMPUTER MODEL OF PHOEBE'S STRUCTURE, AND THIS SHOWED THEM THAT PHOEBE CAME FROM A REGION OF SPACE FAR BEYOND THE PLANET NEPTUNE, CALLED THE KUIPER BELT.

Saturn's Rings

Saturn is surrounded by a huge system of beautiful rings. Before *Cassini* could orbit Saturn, it had to pass through the gap between two rings to the other side. In the process, it discovered new moons and data about the rings never revealed before.

The Rings

Saturn's rings are wide, thin bands of particles that orbit the planet. Each ring is up to thousands of miles wide, but less than 3,200 feet (1 km) thick, and some are only 30 feet (10 m) thick.

Saturn's turquoise rings consist of pure water ice, while the reddish rings contain other chemicals.

Saturn has seven main rings and together they cover 169,000 miles (273,266 km) of space. They would stretch across three-quarters of the distance between Earth and its moon! The space between the rings is filled with a haze of tiny particles of dust.

As *Cassini* passed between the rings, it took amazingly clear, closeup pictures of them. The images showed that the rings are mostly made of particles of frozen water and dust from **meteoroids**. Most of the particles are tiny but some are 0.5 miles (0.8 km) long. The particles and structures knock and collide with one another, creating waves, spirals, and glittering trails, like the wake of a moving ship.

Interactive Moons

Cassini discovered new moons among the rings, some of which were collecting particles from the rings. Scientists now think that the darker particles in the rings come from dark rocks on Phoebe and Iapetes, another captured moon. One thing is certain, the data collected by *Cassini* shows that these beautiful rings are even more exciting than scientists dared to hope.

Titan: Cassini Prepares

In October 2004, *Cassini-Huygens* began to focus on the biggest part of the robots' mission, landing the robot *Huygens* on Saturn's moon Titan.

Why Titan?

Scientists were very interested in Titan. It is Saturn's largest moon and the only one to have a thick atmosphere. Scientists knew that the atmosphere contained methane and many other organic compounds that could be associated with life. Titan is also the only moon in the solar system that is known to have clouds. Mission control wanted to find out what was below those clouds!

On October 26, 2004, *Cassini* flew close to Titan, just 750 miles (1,200 km) above its surface. The robot's cameras took pictures of the atmosphere and its radar instruments "saw" through the clouds to record the surface. These images were transmitted to mission control. They helped the scientists to choose *Huygens*'s landing site.

In December, *Cassini-Huygens* turned toward Titan and prepared to release *Huygens*. Until then, *Huygens* had played almost no part in the mission. During the long seven-year journey, this small robot had been in a deep sleep, although it was "woken" every six months to check that it was still working. On December 17, 2004, *Cassini-Huygens* headed directly toward Titan. On December 25, the robotic probe was separated from *Cassini*.

Cassini's radar took this photo of Titan. It shows huge lakes below the thick atmosphere.

SPACE FIRST

THE SEPARATION OF *HUYGENS* FROM *CASSINI* HAPPENED INCREDIBLY FAST, IN JUST 0.15 SECOND. AS THE ELECTRICAL CONNECTORS WERE SEPARATED, TWO EXPLOSIVE BOLTS WERE FIRED AND THEY TRIGGERED SPRINGS, RAMPS, AND ROLLERS TO DETACH AND PUSH *HUYGENS* AWAY. SCIENTISTS IN MISSION CONTROL WAITED ANXIOUSLY TO SEE WHETHER THE FIRST ROBOT LANDING MILLIONS OF MILES AWAY WOULD BE SUCCESSFUL.

Huygens Touches Down

When *Cassini* released *Huygens*, the probe was more than 2 million miles (nearly 4 million km) from Titan. For 20 days, the robot cruised toward Titan, reaching its atmosphere on January 14, 2005. None of its instruments were working yet, except a clock set to wake up the robot 15 minutes before reaching Titan's atmosphere.

As *Huygens* entered Titan's atmosphere 789 miles (1,270 km) above the ground, it began to fall fast and became very hot. Without its heat shield, its instruments would have been destroyed in temperatures that reached 3,000 degrees Fahrenheit (1,700 °C).

An artist shows how *Huygens* dropped by parachute onto Titan.

When the robot had dropped to 105 miles (170 km) above the ground, its main parachute opened and its speed slowed, while its heat shield fell away. A smaller parachute then opened to bring the robot gently down to land.

Collecting Data

Huygens carried batteries that would allow it to transmit to *Cassini* for three hours while it dropped through Titan's atmosphere. Some of *Huygens* scientific instruments immediately began to collect and transmit data to *Cassini*. The gas chemical analyzer and the aerosol collector took samples of the gases and dust particles in the atmosphere. These were later analyzed to show that the atmosphere was mostly nitrogen (as on Earth) but that the clouds were composed of methane.

Once the parachutes opened, *Huygens*'s wind instrument recorded how the robot was pushed and blown first one way and then another. For the final 90 miles (150 km) of the drop, cameras took photographs in all directions. Just before the robot landed, it switched on a lamp so that its instrument could photograph the landing site just before *Huygens* touched down.

SPACE FIRST

FOUR HOURS AND 36 MINUTES AFTER *HUYGENS* BEGAN TRANSMITTING, *CASSINI* TURNED TO POINT ITS LARGE ANTENNA TOWARD EARTH. THE SIGNALS TRAVELED AT THE SPEED OF LIGHT, BUT SATURN IS SO FAR FROM EARTH IT TOOK THEM ONE HOUR AND SEVEN MINUTES TO REACH MISSION CONTROL. THE SCIENTISTS WERE AMAZED TO SEE THAT THE FLAT, ORANGE-COLORED SURFACE OF TITAN LOOKED JUST LIKE ARIZONA!

Amazing Titan

Huygens's mission was incredibly successful. The robot fell through the atmosphere for 2.5 hours, collecting and transmitting data to *Cassini* through the Entry Assembly Module. The images revealed an extraordinary landscape that looked similar to Earth but, as the data later showed, was very different in many ways. Even after landing, *Huygens* continued to analyze and transmit data for an additional 30 minutes.

Riverbeds, Lakes, and Rocks

If you could stand on Titan, you would see ranges of hills, with narrow channels running down the hillsides and joining together to form rivers. Although the rivers and lakes were dry when *Huygens* photographed them, the shape of the land showed that running liquid had worn away the land and run into lakes and seas.

Titan's temperature is very different to that on Earth. Titan is extremely cold with the temperature staying a steady −290 degrees Fahrenheit (−180 °C).

This is an artist's impression of Titan based on the data gathered by *Huygens*.

The land is frozen water ice, not rocks, and the seas are filled with liquid methane. Like water on Earth, methane on Titan exists in all three states of matter, solid, liquid, and gas. If you looked up at Titan's sky, you would see clouds of methane vapor. *Huygens* recorded drops of methane rain that fell on the robot.

Research Continued

Huygens's descent was so smooth, the robot was able to analyze the ground it landed on before its batteries failed. The data showed that *Huygens* had touched down on an area scattered with rounded cobblestones of solid water ice. Research did not stop when *Huygens*'s batteries failed. *Cassini* made many more flybys of Titan, taking images of different areas of ground. Some of these images have led scientists to think there might be a large ocean beneath Titan's surface.

Extraordinary Moons

After leaving Titan, *Cassini* journeyed to other moons of Saturn. In 2005, for example, the robot photographed and flew past Enceladus and Iapetus, two moons that particularly interested scientists. *Cassini*'s whole mission was so successful that in 2008, it was extended, first to 2010, and then to 2017. This allowed *Cassini* to return to some moons and to explore others.

Bright Enceladus

Enceladus is Saturn's brightest moon because it is covered by water ice, which reflects almost all of the sun's light. Scientists were excited because *Cassini*'s images of its south pole showed several stripes, which they nicknamed "tiger stripes," and which they thought might be caused by earthquakes. In 2005, when *Cassini* returned for a closer look, it photographed a huge plume of ice

plumes

Scientists created this model of Enceladus from data collected by *Cassini*.

oceans

and steam shooting out from Enceladus's south pole. *Cassini* later found evidence of a watery ocean beneath Enceladus's surface, where scientists think **microbes** may exist.

Iapetus

Scientists sent *Cassini* to examine Iapetus because they wanted to know why part of its surface is always dark, not because it is night there, but because its dark material does not reflect light. Analysis showed that the material is dust. Scientists think it may have come from the moon Phoebe, which is also dark. The rest of Iapetus's surface is much brighter, with many craters and a chain of mountains about 33,000 feet (10 km) high. They are located around its equator, a horizontal region around the moon's center.

Mimas and Rhea

Mimas and Rhea have more craters than any other moon in the solar system. *Cassini* photographed Mimas several times, including its huge 88-mile (140 km) wide crater. The robot also found evidence that Mimas had been created by sucking up material from Saturn's rings, leaving a gap 2,980 miles (4,800 km) wide between the "A" and "B" rings.

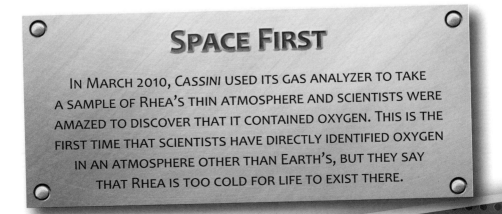

SPACE FIRST

In March 2010, *Cassini* used its gas analyzer to take a sample of Rhea's thin atmosphere and scientists were amazed to discover that it contained oxygen. This is the first time that scientists have directly identified oxygen in an atmosphere other than Earth's, but they say that Rhea is too cold for life to exist there.

Stormy Saturn

After *Cassini*'s mission was extended in 2010, to 2017, the robot orbited Saturn another 155 times. This allowed scientists to study Saturn's atmosphere and see how it changed as the seasons slowly changed. Saturn takes 29.5 Earth-years to orbit the sun, which means that *Cassini* will have collected data over two seven-year seasons.

Saturn's atmosphere is about 97 percent hydrogen, with the remainder being mostly helium, which is a type of gas. The lower part of the atmosphere contains thick clouds, and this is where Saturn's weather is generated. The highest clouds are

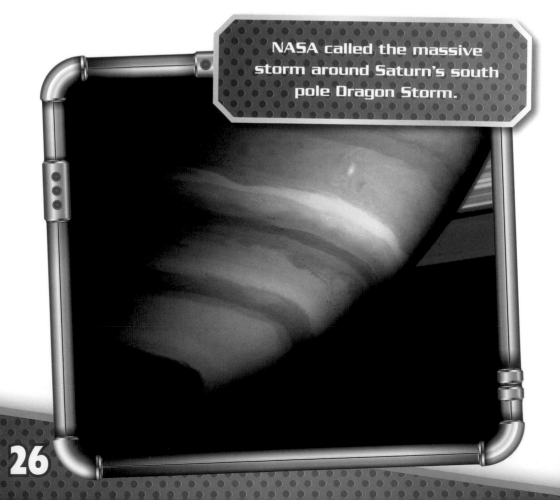

NASA called the massive storm around Saturn's south pole Dragon Storm.

mainly **ammonia**, and the lowest clouds are water. *Cassini*'s remote instruments were able to look through the thick clouds to analyze the planet below. There, the pressure of the atmosphere is so huge it squeezes the hydrogen gas, turning it to liquid hydrogen and then, lower in the atmosphere, to liquid helium. Scientists think Saturn may have a rocky core that is 10 times the size of Earth.

Stormy Weather

This huge planet is extremely windy, with winds of up to 1,118 miles (1,800 km) per hour, more than four times as fast as Earth's strongest tornado. The strong winds are caused by the incredibly fast speed at which Saturn spins on its axis. It makes one spin (one Saturn-day) every 10.6 hours! *Cassini*'s Composite Infrared Spectrometer has recorded many hurricane-like storms around the planet's north and south poles.

Massive Thunderstorm

On December 5, 2010, *Cassini* picked up signals of a massive thunderstorm that burst through Saturn's atmosphere. Huge flashes of lightning and clouds of water ice and ammonia were blown all around the northern half of the planet. Scientists think that a superstorm like this one probably occurs every year on Saturn (every 30 Earth-years).

SCIENCE FIRST

CASSINI'S SPACE ADVENTURE IS SET TO COME TO AN END ON SEPTEMBER 15, 2017, BUT BEFORE IT DOES IT WILL EXPLORE THE SPACE BETWEEN SATURN AND ITS INNERMOST RING. FROM LATE 2016, IT WILL COLLECT DATA CLOSE TO SATURN'S ATMOSPHERE AND TAKE PHOTOS OF ITS OLDEST RINGS. THEN IT WILL PLUNGE INTO SATURN'S ATMOSPHERE WHERE IT WILL BE DESTROYED.

Mission Complete?

Cassini's missions to Saturn were stunningly successful, with most of its objectives fulfilled. In 2017, *Cassini* itself will be destroyed as it drops through Saturn's atmosphere, but the data and images it has produced will continue to be examined. New questions will arise, for which scientists will look for answers.

Incredible Achievements

Between 2004 and 2014, *Cassini*, the robot orbiter, traveled 2 billion miles (3.2 billion km), during which it made 206 orbits, including 132 close flybys of Saturn's moons. It took 332,000 photos and collected 514 GB of scientific data. Hundreds of scientists have been analyzing the images and data, and more than 3,000 scientific papers have already been written and published.

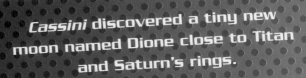

Cassini discovered a tiny new moon named Dione close to Titan and Saturn's rings.

SPACE DISCOVERIES

THESE ARE SOME OF THE MANY DISCOVERIES OF CASSINI-HUYGENS:

- 31 NEW MOONS AND SEVERAL NEW RINGS
- SEAS, LAKES, AND RIVERBEDS ON TITAN'S SURFACE, WHICH ARE FILLED NOT WITH WATER BUT WITH LIQUID METHANE
- COMPLEX PARTICLES IN TITAN'S ATMOSPHERE, INCLUDING BENZENE AND VARIOUS PLASTICS
- TOWERING FOUNTAINS OF WATER ICE ON THE MOON ENCELADUS, SUGGESTING THE PRESENCE OF AN UNDERGROUND SEA
- IAPETUS'S DARK LUNAR AREAS EXPLAINED BY THE PRESENCE OF DARK, REDDISH DUST
- A MASSIVE CRATER ON THE MOON MIMAS
- POLAR STORMS ON SATURN AND A SUPERSTORM THAT SPREAD AROUND THE NORTHERN HALF OF THE PLANET

New discoveries, however, lead to new questions and the search for answers. In 2011, NASA funded the development of a robot lander called Titan Mare Explorer (TiME) to explore one of Titan's seas. This robot boat would be the first to sail on a sea beyond Earth. However, space missions are so expensive NASA cannot fund them all, and in 2013, TiME was canceled for now.

Will Astronauts Ever Go to Saturn?

Cassini has proven how efficient robots are at collecting and transmitting data. The idea of astronauts visiting Saturn's moons is immensely exciting, but such a mission could take place only in the distant future. The length of the journey, providing supplies for astronauts, and returning them safely to Earth are far beyond our current technical abilities. In the meantime, space robots are helping us discover more about the wonders of our solar system!

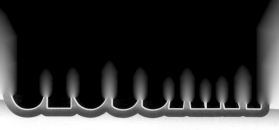

ammonia A strong-smelling substance made when the gases nitrogen and hydrogen combine.

antennae Devices that send and receive radio signals.

asteroids Lumps of rock in space. Many orbit the sun in a band between Mars and Jupiter.

atmosphere A layer of gases that surround a planet or moon.

craters Large holes in the ground caused when something crashes into the surface.

data Information.

filters Fine meshes that separate larger particles from smaller ones.

flyby When a spacecraft flies close to a planet or moon in order to gain extra momentum from it.

generators Machines that produce electricity.

hydrogen A substance that is usually a gas on Earth, but can exist as a liquid if the temperature is cold enough.

meteoroids Rocky particles traveling through space.

microbes Bacteria and other tiny forms of life.

mission control Scientists, technicians, and other people in charge of a space mission.

momentum A combination of mass and speed produced by a moving object. Momentum acts to keep an object moving.

orbiter A spacecraft that travels through space, but does not land.

orbiting Traveling around an object in a circular way.

particles Tiny pieces of matter.

probe A robot that is programmed to explore a particular area of space.

robots Machines that are programmed to carry out particular jobs.

sensors Devices that react to particular aspects of the environment, such as light waves.

thruster engines Small engines that are used to change the direction or speed of a spacecraft.

FOR MORE INFORMATION

Books

Carson, Mary Kay and Ron Miller. *How Many Planets Circle the Sun?*
New York, NY: Sterling Children's Books, 2014.

Dugan, Christine. *Space Exploration* (TIME for Kids).
Huntington Beach, CA: Teacher Created Materials, 2012.

Simon, Seymour. *Our Solar System*. New York, NY:
HarperCollins, 2014.

Squire, Ann O. *Planet Saturn* (New True Books: Space).
Danbury CT: Children's Press, 2014.

Websites

Due to the changing nature of Internet links, PowerKids Press has developed an online list of websites related to the subject of this book. This site is updated regularly. Please use this link to access the list: **www.powerkidslinks.com/res/cassini**